BUILDING BRITAIN'S CANALS

BUILDING BRITAIN'S CANALS

by
DAVID GLADWIN

K.A.F. BREWIN BOOKS
STUDLEY 1988

First published by
Brewin Books Ltd, Studley, Warwickshire.
November 1988
Reprinted June 1990
Reprinted May 1991
Reprinted October 1993
Reprinted April 1996
Reprinted July 2001
Reprinted March 2006

www.brewinbooks.com

ISBN 1 85858 069 2

Typeset in Baskerville and
made and printed in Great Britain
by Supaprint (Redditch) Ltd., Redditch, Worcestershire.
www.supaprint.com

AUTHOR'S NOTE

Born alongside the river Thames and being brought up in the Essex marshes has left David Gladwin with a marked affinity to water and it is not surprising, therefore, that a number of his occupations have been connected with the sea or inland waters. As one of a team involved in transportation research and development he finds that waterway people have changed very little in their enthusiasm for the subject and a waterborne way of life. Not only does this make research a pleasure but ensures that the faceless ones who would wish to destroy the priceless artifacts that so enhance the waterways scene are prevented from doing so. As an example consider the waterway preservation societies without whom we would have little of the canal system left. As a generality they are run by and employ in the works perfectly ordinary people, people who use their skills to the best advantage in the field of restoration and by so doing maintain the individuality of their local waterway. This book is therefore designed to appeal to anyone who, like the author, finds the charm of waterways lies as much in the particular as in the whole, and who seek to appreciate and conserve a two hundred year old way of life.

BOOKS BY THE SAME AUTHOR

English Canals (The Oakwood Press)
Canals of the Welsh Valleys (The Oakwood Press)
Passenger Boats on Inland Waterways (The Oakwood Press)
British Waterways (Spur Books)
The Canals of Britain (B.T. Batsford)
The Waterways of Britain, A Social Panorama (B.T. Batsford)
Victorian & Edwardian Canals (B.T. Batsford)
A Pictorial History of Canals (B.T. Batsford)
Steam on the Road (B.T. Batsford)

CONTENTS

INTRODUCTION

The main difficulty inherent in assembling the illustrations for this book lay in the fact that photography came too late to record the building of the greater part of Britain's waterway network and, therefore, recourse has had to be made to artists' impressions.

Nowadays, re-building is the theme and photographs depicting regeneration of 'lost' canals have been chosen to show as far as possible the methods involved in these works. Some artifacts — gate-collars, paddle-gearing, even warehouses — are virtually unaltered and where this is so modern illustrations have been drawn upon. It must be remembered though, today is an historical event by tomorrow.

Some photographs included may not have great artistic merit, being in all probability taken by a canal labourer with frozen fingers using a box camera, but — and it is a big but — they are unique and irreplaceable.

As far as possible copyright credits have been checked but if, inadvertently, and unknowingly, errors have been made, advice of these would be appreciated in order that they may be corrected in later editions.

Vogue la galère!

A BRIEF HISTORY

The earliest known waterways in England are those built by the Romans, mainly for the transport of food from the hinterland but also to assist the movement of troops. Excavations carried out in 1947 have established the original cross-section of the Caerdyke (in use at least from 50-60 AD) as being 13.7m (45ft) wide at top, 9m (30ft) at bottom and at least 1.5m (5ft) deep — comparable with many canals in use today.

Although vast numbers of short artificial navigations were constructed over the next 1,500 years they were, in the main, by-passes to bends of rivers or extensions serving to supply Abbeys or Manor houses with food and fuel during the few months of the summer when rivers were navigable in their natural state.

One of the first pound locks similar to todays, inasmuch as it was described as having two pairs of gates ("double doores") was built on the River Lea in 1580 but the older and far more hazardous 'flash locks' lingered on into the 20th century. Possibly first utilised a thousand years ago, these latter were basically gated weirs which divided rivers into lengths or pounds. Normally kept closed to raise the water level above the lock they were opened by either swinging the single gate bodily or removing sections of the weirs. An upcoming barge would, on the pent water being released and a new level formed, go as far as possible assisted by great teams of men and, in later days, horses until it grounded and had to wait the next 'flash'; while a barge moving downhill would 'ride' the flash — in all an incredibly hazardous proceeding. These structures were crude and regularly destroyed by floods, while in time of drought or frost they were unusable.

The first completely new work in the modern style was, with the exception of the Exeter Ship canal (arguably first completed with pound locks c. 1564), in Ireland where for the twin purposes of ameliorating unemployment and assisting land reclamation the Newry canal from the Tyrone Collieries on Lough Neagh via the Bann river and an entirely artificial cut to the town of Newry, was commenced in 1730, being completed in 1742 under the guidance of a "noted engineer', Thomas Steers. For the period, the whole length of navigation, 29km (18m) was a considerable feat of engineering. Fifteen pound locks, each 13.4m (44ft) long and 4.7m (15ft 6in) wide, had a rise (or fall!) of some 3m (10ft), serving to control the water flow.

However, the advantages of this waterway were not realised in the remainder of the United Kingdom and the next, the St. Helens canal, although vastly advantageous to the population of its area, initially caused surprisingly little external reaction. Running 11.26km (7m) from the River Mersey it was a strictly industrial waterway carrying coal from the collieries in South Lancashire to feed the evaporators at the saltworks and moving processed salt both to the Liverpool docks for export and towards the rising populations of Lancashire and Yorkshire. When this (and the later Duke of Bridgewater's canal) was seen to be a success, and it had been hailed as a symbol of a new age, the public rushed to subscribe to all and every scheme proposed. The Chairman of the Ellesmere canal reported in 1805 that "the books were opened about noon, and ere sun set a million of money was confided to the care of the Committee" — I wonder if people would volunteer to pay so willingly for motorways today?

Unfortunately, except for canals which were relatively quickly finished, one major factor intervened to change the rosy glow of a new dawn to a hangover. There were simply too many vacancies chasing too few skilled engineers and the available labour force. Even when the directors of a new waterway found their engineer he might not do more than make an occasional visit, leaving the work to his pupils, who were of variable quality, one even admitting ". . . I have been cheated by undertakers and clerks and am unlucky enough to know it. The work done is slovenly, our workmen are bad and I am not sufficiently strict . . ."; although others, fortunately for us today, were far better.

Contracts on early canals were truly handed out in 'penny-packets' — perhaps a dozen bridges, ten locks or as little as 100m (110 yds) of earthworks. Even an aqueduct might be handled in two parts with Smith doing the masonry and Brown the channel. Locks might be split into separate contracts for the brick-, iron- and wood-work. Who got the contract depended on many factors, but basically the proprietors, naturally, wanted the cheapest while the top-class engineer, with one eye to his reputation, and perhaps conscience, wanted the best. The contract placed, the contractor would have to find his navvies — the pick and shovel mob — and no matter how fast the cattle-boats brought them over from the Irish bogs there still remained a shortage with, to add to the engineers worries, bitter complaints of men being "stolen away for 5p (one shilling) a day". Tradesmen, the blacksmiths, carpenters and bricklayers, were a different matter as they existed in every village, howbeit they too had to be weaned away by the offer of better wages and they rarely came wholly entirely under the control of the contractor — when the landowner required work done to the windows of the 'Big House' then the carpenter might be seen no more, thus holding up the whole works.

Even when these shortages did not arise, or were eliminated, weather could cause unforeseen delays and extra costs. On the Monkland canal one contractor quoted 1p per m^3 (1 3/4d per cubic yard) of soil removed; after a fortnight's rain the resident engineer, James Watt, reckoned it was costing the man nearly double this sum for labour alone. Although a contract and specification might be meticulously drawn up and agreed, the contractor was reliant upon outside suppliers for his materials including bricks, and as time meant money everything that was sent was used whether good or not. In the case of the Birmingham & Fazeley canal terse comments were contained in a report that ". . . such bad bricks were used they could scarce find enough for fronts . . ."; that others were laid without mortar; while puddling, far from being of best blue clay, "Clearly picked over, and free from stones etc.", comprised soil, gravel and sand. Elsewhere the locks at Wolverhampton, like indeed many others, were shoddily built with the great Brindley reporting ". . . the wood work was ill tenanted & Mortized" and the ironwork, again from an outside source, had such bad "teeth & pinions" that it would have to be altered.

However, the necessity of patching and repairing canals over the last two hundred years, coupled with the original idiosyncrasies, has left us with a magnificent legacy; variety in every detail allied to often superb and always fascinating engineering.

THE TRACK

The track carries the lifeblood of the waterways: water. By it's nature to be controllable water must be kept level, or as James Brindley succinctly put it "laid on his back".

Ideally, and had it been possible within the engineering knowledge of the time, each and every canal would have an enormously long summit with the locks concentrated nearest to a junction with another waterway or at the seaward end, thus turning the top level into one vast linear reservoir. Since the ideal was unattainable Brindley's technique, also emulated by his pupils who, between them, must have overseen the building of half of the deadwater navigations, of allowing a canal to meander along a convenient contour line had much to commend it. Time was, initially, hardly a factor to cause any concern — as long as the goods got to the factory regularly it was the continuity that was (and still is) important, not speed — and if by twisting and turning half-a-dozen extra villages, each with a wharf and trade demand (however small) could be served, so much the better. Furthermore on a tonne/km toll basis greater income could accrue! It is also true that although greater land purchase costs were incurred, earthworks, whether cuttings or embankments, were relatively small and the navvies' labour cost reduced thereby. Even so, tunnels, aqueducts and similar works were unavoidable, although now with greater surveying facilities available we know, for example, that Harecastle tunnel could have been avoided by a slight diversion of the canal line. Later waterways, either faced with railway competition or built in the railway age, are far more direct and purposeful than their 'agricultural' forebears. The sole reason for their existence was factory-city-dock trade — import and export, with the drawback that, like today's motorways, villages were bypassed and speed the guiding principle.

CONTROLLED WATERS

Having laid the water on his back, the problem then is how to carry him up and down a hill. The basic principle is to provide a water staircase but every drop of water that flows downhill is lost from the summit (without the provision of expensive back pumping) and engineers have sought to find means of economising in its usage. Over seventy patent specifications relating to locks were filed between 1775 and 1830, including 'balancing locks', compressed air operation, giant ping-pong balls and hot air balloons to hoist the boats and a multitude of lifts or inclined planes. The building and operational costs of most would have been higher than back pumping even had they been practicable.

The size of locks was governed by three factors, all seemingly of equal importance. These were the desire of the engineer to settle for a standard gauge thus allowing through boat movements, the availability of water and the cost (land, material and labour) of the works. Unfortunately each engineer had different ideas of which standard should be adhered to. The varying lock dimensions eventually proved to be the canal network Achilles heel and today still precludes the use of a boat exceeding 14m (46ft) long x 2.08m (6ft 10in) wide x 0.69m (2ft 3in) draught, if it is to traverse the entire system.

OVER AND UNDER

There were innumerable permutations available to the engineer who had to build bridges. The materials included stone, brick, wood and iron, they could be fixed, swing, lift, rolling or clap and if those did not suffice aqueducts and tunnels were other possibilities open to them, albeit not entirely from choice.

However, while the engineer could lay down guide-lines, the eventual appearance of the bridge was in the hands of the contractors and even before some waterways were opened failures of quite large structures were not unknown, with gloomy engineers' reports no doubt making shareholders' faces even more lachrymose. In 1789 the "Ruins of the Coventry Com^{ys} Aqueduct at the River Tame" were part of a sightseeing tour and on the Grand Junction the failure of Wolverton aqueduct over the river Ouse, whose leaks had been so bad as to be nicknamed "the tears of the contractors", caused the reinstatement of the old locks whereby boats had to drop down the valley and climb up the other side.

So far as bridges are concerned the Stratford-on-Avon canal must have the greatest mixture of the network, reflecting the number of engineers employed in the works, and include one swing, three draw and a mixture of split iron and orthodox brick bridges. Like many other waterways, the monogram of the company — S.C.C. — is to be found on gate anchors and, less usually, on the ironwork of some of the small accommodation bridges. Many iron bridges are misleading for the maker's name will be emblazoned large with the date although this latter may not be at all accurate. Relatively few ironworks tendered for, or undertook, such assemblies as the cost of making the mould was probably not justified for the small quantities ordered at one time. Therefore whichever ironworks was involved tended to cast the components of an extra 'stock' bridge or two all bearing the same date.

In the relatively affluent early days of canal building very attractive plates were cast for attachment to brick bridges, showing both names and numbers of which those on the Staffordshire & Worcestershire Canal are best known, mainly for their quaint names — Giggetty, Falling Sands, Round Hill, Clay House, Green's Forge, Bumble Hole, Mops Farm, Castle Croft, Moat House and Mitton Chapel — and although subsequently decimated by local and boat-borne vandals, the British Waterways Board, to their credit, have replaced the missing ones with cast replicas.

G.R. Jebb, engineer of the Birmingham Canal Navigations, reported in 1888 that "... The effect of mining operations on bridges is very disastrous ... Arches very soon succumb, and are invariably replaced by flat tops of iron or timber, which can be easily raised by either screw or hydraulic jacks ...". Small cast plates were designed for use with these, incorporating the initials of the canal company and the name of the bridge or junction. The bulk of these have, unfortunately, disappeared although a few relics are to be found here and there, having an industrial charm — Hempole, Pratts and Monument Lane with a Jibbet thrown in for good measure. Some, carrying no name, have instead the building or re-building date in Roman numerals: MDCCCXXI probably baffled many a boatman who knew it best as 'Slaughterhouse'. But the bulk of waterways disdained such unnecessary expenditure, settling instead for a mere number, howbeit this might have the curliest figures available from the foundry.

ALL HAD A PURPOSE

The buildings which were built alongside or straddling a waterway were of the greatest importance, particularly from the engineering aspect. A canal company when seeking its authorising Act of Parliament had to give assurances that fair trade was its intended way of life, with every man, whether a single boat owner or employee of a large carrier, having the right to his share of wharfage, warehousing and other canalside facilities. Parliament was, however, somewhat sceptical and while giving the canal companies the right to build warehouses laid down a standard charge (on average roughly 0.4p per tonne for the first 10 days, thereafter 2½p per tonne) but also often forced a clause on the company to the effect that if they failed to build warehouses local landowners could do so instead but having "always to meet the reasonable demands of maintenance of banks etc."

Undoubtedly, the most efficient (and therefore attractive) form is that found where the warehouse straddles the waterway with hatches cut in the floor to allow loading or discharge of goods but, even if more commonplace, terminal 'box' warehouses now have a charm if only that of mellow age. Other less conspicuous structures, were those used by the canal companies servants; lock- and toll-houses, stables and hovels. By contrast, when canal trade was booming, many manufactories were built astride an arm of the waterway — a statement made in 1837 describes all too well how these buildings caused the massive water pollution so common until recently. "It [the factory] is a hell-hole, that not even the canal water can cool, for that, itself, boils".

Very noticeable among photographs of, for example, interchange stations, is the lack of provision for the men employed there; one religious society spent quite considerable sums of money putting up stables to shelter horses but did nothing to alleviate the plight of the boatmen or canal workers.

BOLTS & DOWELS

It is to the maintenance man, whether employed by the British Waterways Board or other similar bodies, that the sins or omissions of our contracting forebears become most obvious and it is not altogether inapposite that the majority of large jobs are passed over to today's contracting firms. Unfortunately, while today's maintenance men undoubtedly have the expertise they are deficient both in number and plant, the former because wages and conditions are both below the standards a working man may reasonably expect and the latter because capital investment has been insufficient for many, many years.

On one canal in the 1920s the first mechanical pump brought into use was greatly acclaimed — but it was powered by an early De Dion 2½ h.p. car engine which the Superintendent had acquired from the local schoolmaster.

The employees of canal companies or for that matter of the British Waterways Board now, rarely indulge in demarcation disputes and it is salutory to reflect on the wide variety of work that was — and is — carried out by both tradesmen and labourers. The late George Bate, foreman carpenter, Worcester & Birmingham canal, and an employee for 57 years: "A years' work? 1924 for instance, I prepared the timber for the stop groove cill and sheet piling at Tardebigge Dry Dock, made two bottom gates (Lock 32) and two top gates (3 and 55) and made a new shed for Wychall Reservoir. In 1925 I repaired the Stop [safety] Gates at Selly Oak Bridge, assisted at putting in the new timber wharf at Cadburys, Bournville, made new bottom gates for Lock 52 and a top gate for 40. I also spent a month piling between locks 51 and 52, helped to fix the dams at Withybed Green, Alvechurch, when the bottom of the canal started leaking and we had to drain it, put in the [still extant] paling fence and gates at the Saw Mill in the [Tardebigge] Yard, and then spent a cold old six weeks — November to December — repairing the gates of locks 1 to 5 on the Droitwich Junction Canal". In the next year he "only" built and installed four gates, fixed a style and made more fencing. In 1927 he made and fitted a new swing bridge at Diglis Basin, dismantled a timber crane, made and fitted five gates, plus "assisting to lift steam tug *Birmingham* sunk at Kings Norton tunnel".

In bygone days the foreman-carpenter of a waterway, a virtually autonomous being, was also responsible for what we now call 'quality control'. One mentioned a baulk of 0.6m (24 in) square and 3.35m (11ft) long being brought, first by a Yorkshire Steam Tractor 8km (5m) from the felling site to the wharf, and thence by horse-boat 30-odd kilometers (20 miles or so) up the canal, only for it to be rejected by, initially, the steam sawyer, confirmed by the carpenter, for having heart-rot "no wider than a 10p piece!"

Nowadays lock gates for the nationalised waterways are mass produced in factories and it is only some restoration groups who have the experience of actually making them. Even so, the process of lock-gate making differs considerably from that of yesteryear. To quote one item, all nuts and bolts were made by the canal company's own blacksmith, and long after the virtual standardisation of Whitworth thread elsewhere he continued to use the taps and dies of his predecessor as there was no need for fittings to be interchangeable with others outside of his 'own' waterway. All wood was seasoned prior to working, but despite that, all holes were bored 3mm (1/8th in) undersize and the bolts were driven in by sledge-hammers. An apprentice was given this job and such was the bite of 305mm (12in) thick oak that he could drive no more than three or four in a day. Similarly, the mortice and tennon joint at the head were rather more than an exact fit and although the balance beams were always offered up in the workshops, they were a wretchedly hard job to refit in situ.

The older canal carpenters were (and some still are) adept at 'make do and mend' and problems were usually overcome as they were faced. At Offerton Lock (No.11), Worcester & Birmingham canal, a gate built in 1900 was temporarily replaced in May 1940 by 'lending' one from elsewhere, while [George Bate] ". . . the old gate was transported to Tardebigge [workshops]. I repaired it by fitting a new heel, short splice on the head and a second-hand balance beam". Thus renewed it then lasted another thirty-two years.

1.   It was of vital importance for any canal company to have a good outlet for the trade on its banks.   The Grand Surrey carried this philosophy even further by eventually turning most of their waterway into docks. The extent of the works can be gauged by this illustration of Surrey Docks, but apart from the use of steam, methods of building were those of the great days of canal building.

Port of London Authority

13

2.)　　The Manchester Ship Canal was the last and finest navigation to be built in Britain.　Much as the Bridge-
3.)　　water had come about as the result of the intransigence of the old river navigation proprietors, so the Bridgewater Trustees allowed their waterway to stagnate after 1842, and the merchants found it cheaper to rail goods to Hull and ship from there rather than via Liverpool.　Two plans were proposed, one for a tidal navigation 42 miles (67 km) long, and the other, designed by E. Leader Williams, was for the line adopted,

(2) shows the normal method used to start the work.　British Waterways Board.

with five locks, a navigable depth of 28 feet (8.89m) and 36 miles (58km) long. Within a decade of the opening, 1st January 1894, the S.S. *Manchester City*, 461 feet (140m) long, 52 feet (15.8m) beam, and carrying 7,500 tons of cargo had reached Manchester without mishap. The labour involved in shifting approximately 77 million tons of spoil (one fifth of which was sandstone) can only be described as prodigious.

(3) As soon as a water channel was available steam dredgers were called in to deepen and widen the channel.
Manchester Public Libraries

4.   Skinner's (or Langley's) Weir, River Thames, depicted c.1863.   Included to show a typical river fitting of the eighteenth century, this flash lock and weir, long since gone, was slightly over 1½ miles (2.4km) below Bablock Hythe Ferry.   The charge per barge for a return trip was, in 1793, 15p compared with 1p for a pound lock toll due to the relatively high labour cost involved in working it.   At the same time it was said the weir was 'in very bad repair'.   In 1802, during a survey of the Thames, Robert Mylne found that barges were often forced to tranship goods here into a spare boat kept for the purpose, and that a poundlock should supercede 'this outmoded scheme'.   The Fish Inn, 'a thatched cottage offering repose and refreshment', was last held by Joe Skinner, known familiarly as 'Old Joe' and he is the gentleman on the left of the photograph. The whole area was altered when a new cut was made 1896-99.

Oxfordshire County Library

5.   This engraving is based on an unreproducable, undated, sketch, which is believed to depict workmen on the Caledonian canal.   Certainly it fits very well a description of 1804 when '. . . observing how carelessly the labourers were dabbling with their pick and spades, and how apt they were to look around them at everything which was to be seen; while others were winding slowly out with each a little gravel in a wheelbarrow . . .' the commentator doubted whether the waterway would ever be finished.   However, it is one of the very few drawings of the period to survive; the few men at work may explain why the Caledonian took so long to complete!

J.K. Ebblewhite

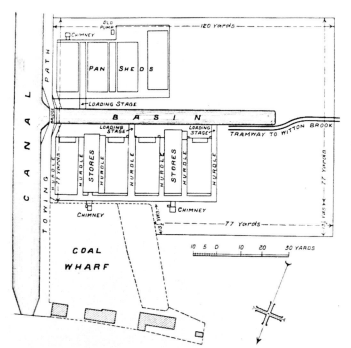

THE LATE MR. ROBERT WILLIAMSON
SALT WORKS, WINCHAM.

6.   The fundamental reason underlying the original growth of the canal network was the desire of manu-factories to have an easier supply of raw materials for the works and, equally, a wider market for the finished products.   With a little careful planning it was possible not only to increase profits but, using this cheap transport medium, to reduce prices which again enhanced sales.   The Salt Works at Wincham have taken full advantage of the water facilities available on the Trent & Mersey canal with every item from pansheds to coal wharf conveniently located.   Nevertheless the very nature of a salt work, relying on a brine pump as the source of raw material, sometimes resulted in it being in a less than favourable position, where the advantages were nullified to some extent by having to tranship coal and salt alike to and from the canal by way of a tramroad.   This extra cost, risk of damage and loss of time were only acceptable as long as no more economic alternative was available — and led to the phenomenal growth in road transport after the first world war.

7.   Standedge tunnel, Huddersfield Narrow canal, was opened in 1811, when it was reported that 'upwards of five hundred people' passed through singing 'Rule Britannia and other patriotic songs', their entry being watched by an estimated 10,000 more.   Closed in 1944 due to rock falls and subsidence it had the smallest cross-section of any main line canal tunnel, and boats had, often enough, to tranship part of their twenty ton load into 'lightening' craft which were kept at each end for that purpose.   No provision was made for a towpath and boats were legged or kicked through, a journey time of two hours or so.   After the closure to commercial traffic inspection boats have passed through from time to time but here a party from the Huddersfield Railway Circle have been photographed en route in 1959; the tight fit of the boat and their method of propulsion (banned for a working boatman) are alike visible.

8.　　There are two hazards involved when rivers are made navigable which although present even on still-water navigations are rarely so impressive in their results.　The first is flooding.　The photograph, taken on Sunday, December 13, 1964 shows Dane Street in Northwich.　During that day and the previous one an estimated 300 million gallons of rainwater fell within a five mile radius of Northwich alone, causing the rivers Weaver and Dane to reach almost hitherto unknown levels.　British Waterways' men held the waters back on the upper half of the Weaver above Northwich and by raising all available paddles drained the lower half into the Mersey thus dropping the level of the Dane and reducing the possible damage to Northwich.

British Waterways Board

9.   The river Welland has gone through many vicissitudes in the 500 or so years that it has been 'made navigable' but was always plagued by the other great weakness of river navigations in that it could not offer a twenty-four hours a day water supply, being both tidal — at least as far as Spalding — and prone to drought in summer.   Lighters worked upstream to Deeping and Stamford but Spalding was the great interchange point until trade ceased in the 1930s.   The shafts perched over the stern of the rear-most barge are quants used by the bargemaster and his mate to propel and steer the craft along the river when the wind was unfavourable for sailing.   The weathervane above the centre building designates the one-time greatness and subsequent decline of Spalding inasmuch as it represents a three-masted sailing vessel and is now in the Museum of the Gentlemen's Society.

Gentlemen's Society, Spalding

10. Sheffield & South Yorkshire (River Dun Navigation). The northern rivers even when possible for navigation are large and powerful, calling for wide weirs to allow the escape of flood waters. Even the dumped tyre seems more than life size here at Dalton in 1972.

11.   Another artifact commonly overlooked.   In the case of this type (photographed in the Cromford feeder at Cromford in 1972) it is being superceded, as in common with all other items showing 'Imperial' measures they are being replaced with a metric equivalent as quickly as possible.   Materials used to convey this vital information on water supplies vary from incised stone or iron, brass strips or painted wood.   All have advantages and disadvantages for stone and iron are not easily adjustable should they settle in the bottom of the feeder or go out of alignment, lichen can obscure the figures on stone, brass becomes tarnished with verdigris and oxydises, while wood rots and the markings twixt wind and water disappear.   Plastics can do odd things, one experimental batch is known to have disintegrated in the cold.   Whatever they are manufactured from such gauges are necessary as often the changing water level on a feeder will give advance notice of future flooding along the main watercourse and preventative action can be taken.

12. Breaches in canal banks have a long and melancholy history. They are the result of a number of factors, mainly derived from bad workmanship when the canals were dug, but these inherent weaknesses have been spot-lighted lately as motorised pleasure boats cause infinitely more damage in a year than the relatively gentle movement of horse-boats could in a decade. One outside factor caused this breach near Northwich on the Trent & Mersey canal on July 21, 1907. Continual brine-pumping had undermined the whole area and subsidence on the local navigations, including the river Weaver and Trent & Mersey canal was, and is, both the cause of great concern to local waterways officials and of considerable expense in undertaking remedial works. The boats side are roughly 1.22m (4ft) high from top to bottom, their length 21.3m (70ft) and from this can be estimated the rather frightening extent of the slip. The boat nearest the camera was used for maintenance and has a crane mounted.

24

13.   And on the Manchester, Bolton & Bury, a section of bank weakened by heavy rainfall and with the ground undermined by colliery workings, succumbed, leaving this container boat stranded.   Prestolee.

14.   Jim Bodley, the dredger driver, and his mate, Danny Griffiths, had a rather unusual (if early) Christmas present in 1976.   At the time, the afternoon of Monday, 20th December, they were dredging between Bell's Mill and Newton Bridge, Prestwood, on the Stourbridge canal, when virtually without warning the bed of the waterway fractured and dredger, tug and mudboat, together with an estimated 45 million litres (10 million gallons) of water dropped into the breach.   It is believed the cause was the unfortunate juxtaposition of the dredger's legs and a soft patch of eroded or fissued sandstone which may only have been plugged with debris for many of the years since 1779 when the Stourbridge was opened.   Eventually the breach totalled 7 metres (23ft) in length, with 5.6km (3½m) of the canal being dewatered.

Express & Star, Wolverhampton.

15. Modern camera lenses, while distorting the scene, have the advantage of presenting a panorama within a reasonable compass.   This illustration of the Caldon canal, a branch of the Trent & Mersey, shows all the detail that individually, and as a whole, makes each waterway differ from others.   The skeletal iron foot-bridges, rather spidery balance beams, flat arching over the weir, distinctive cottage and bridge leave the discerning eye with a clear impression of a unified functional and, therefore, beautiful image.   A modern note is added by the presence on the bottom gates of both locks of hydraulic paddle-raising equipment. Nicknamed, not without reason, 'Granny Gearing', it is easy to operate, although having to be wound both up and down it is tediously slow in operation and through this can lead to some difficulties should an emergency arise.   The weir on the left is running, but for all that the level of the pound against the bank seems somewhat high.

British Waterways Board

27

16. A very unusual view of a tunnel, photographed in April 1973 when the Worcester & Birmingham canal was dewatered after a breach had occurred. British Waterway Board's foremen tend to come in two types, the older men who prefer to encourage their men by showing how a shovel should be handled and the younger ones who are probably better in the field of advanced engineering and mechanical handling. As can be seen a good area of Edgbaston tunnel has already been cleared and the nominal depth can be gauged. Built for barges rather than narrow boats, the cross section is impressive. The condition of the wall is all too common and although the opportunity was taken to re-point this stretch much remains to be done but must, perforce, be left until the waterway can again be emptied.

D. James and S. Turner

17. A cast iron milepost of the Monmouthshire Canal Company, which dates back to between the completion of the Monmouthshire canal in 1799 and its later extension finished around 1814, when this record of mileage was superceded upon the whole waterway being remeasured. Quite why it remained in situ is a mystery but there were similar happenings on the Leeds & Liverpool and Bridgwater & Taunton canals, both of which had until quite recently two sets bearing different mileages within a hundred yards or so of one another. It is a tribute to the ironworks who supplied these castings that they have withstood many years of climatic erosion. These fittings were specified in waterways' authorising Acts of Parliament to ensure that mileages — upon which tolls were based — could be easily checked by the carrier or shipper.

NANTWICH 7. MILES.

AUTHERLEY. JUNCTION. 32, MILES.

NORBURY JUNCTION 16½ MILES.

18.   A typical Shropshire Union canal milepost.   Or perhaps it would be more accurate to describe it as a typically Telford milepost, for his roadworks at one time gave their information on cast plates of an identical pattern.   It is interesting to note the varying treatment accorded to the different destinations, but it seems that the foundrymen were often illiterate and relied upon their ability to copy the quillwork of some clerk. It is charitable to assume that inkblots account for the odd fullstops and commas.   A keen eye will often discern mis-spellings or reversed letters on this type of notice although some oddments as 'Gloster', for example, were merely the name commonly used at the time.

30

19.   Leeds & Liverpool canal milepost.   All too often these are well hidden in the verdant countryside growth and may not be found until a maintenance man's slashing hook or powered mower makes contact. Where these are neglected and overgrown to that extent animal and bird life makes itself at home.   On one occasion at this post a wren, when disturbed, flew up expressing her opinion of such an occurrence and proved to have built a nest at the back of the post.   This particular artifact had been partially cleaned prior to photography but on return after a meal break, was found to have new livestock in residence.

J.K. Ebblewhite

20. Very bankrupt canal companies omitted what they considered to be frills, or produced a cheap variant upon a theme. When providing rollers to deflect boats' lines from rubbing on a bridge the Selby proprietors appear to have decided to hang the expense and this, at West Haddlesey, is a fairly typical example of a roller that really rolled. Opened in 1778, the trade on this waterway required 40 or so boats every week but as proof of the roller's efficiency the wear is miniscule. Photographed one shockingly wet day, July 1969.

21. Vandalism has been commonplace since the inception of waterways and was not always the work of mindless morons as all too often it is now. Instead some items were smashed for their scrap value and 'the works interfered with' by road carters who saw their livelihood disappearing. Penalties were severe including ear cropping, whipping and transportation. As the bulk of the population were illiterate a notice like this had little meaning although the phrase 'all people' rather than the orthodox 'Trespassers' is unusual. It stands 10' (3.5m) above ground.

22.   Although taken recently to illustrate modern maintenance methods this photograph is of great interest for all the elements of a typical midland canal are clearly visible, not excluding the industrial scenery.   Single gates are used at both ends of the lock, with ground paddles at the top (to the right of the dumper) but at the bottom and behind the maintenance flat can be seen the twin gate paddles.   The wooden bumper across the weir served mainly to deflect boats across to the lock when windbound, while the surplus water — probably due to a boat working uphill — is running hard down the culverted race.   The lonely paddle in the right foreground can be used either to release flood water or to dewater the pound above the lock for maintenance purposes.   Prior to the introduction of successful steam or motor dredgers it was common practice to close the waterway for a fortnight or so every year while gangs of men shovelled out silt.   Behind and below the lock are the relics of Great Bridge Interchange Basins and of a long-derelict branch.   The basins were rail fed with wagons of coal being off-loaded into boats for onward transmission to factories.   Behind the pile of dirt on the right hand lock wall can be seen a white half-moon shape which contains a waterflow meter, used to gauge the water running to waste.   Birmingham canals, situated as they are on a plateau, have always been advanced in their plans to conserve water; these modern gauges are merely another step along the same road.

British Waterways Board

23.   The Grosvenor canal had its derivation in a typical Thames creek used to supply drinking water to the Chelsea Waterworks Company, but gradually became used by barges until in 1811, Lord Grosvenor, who had his own improvement scheme in mind, agreed to works taking place which eventually materialised as a navigable waterway.   The engineers, consulting and residential, Thomas Cundy and Thomas Thatcher, and the contractors, J & W Johnson and Alexander Brice worked well and the navigation was opened in 1825.   Thereafter it was progressively shortened as land was sold or leased to railway companies, some being used by the London, Brighton & South Coast Railway as they extended Victoria Station until in 1906 the remaining 503 metres (550 yds) was sold to the Westminster Council.   During 1928-9 a new lock and other works were completed at the cost of over £88,000 and the waterway was heavily used for barging domestic and other refuse away to the Thames.   The river entrance to the waterway at low tide is being refurbished prior to the 1928 works.

M. Denney

24. By any standards when the restoration work at present in progress on the Kennet & Avon canal is completed this will truly be a new lamp replacing an old one. It is rather ironical that a number of waterways were only completed with funds supplied by a government anxious to reduce unemployment after the Napoleonic wars, were fettled in the 1930s for a similar reason and, like the Kennet & Avon, are being rehabilitated after yet another slump situation. In 1976 the rebuilding of Lock 11, Widmead flight in the city of Bath, was completed; using a mixture of BWB expertise and Kennet & Avon Canal Trust volunteer labour and contractors' plant. This rejuvenation of a long-derelict flight must have put heart into other restoration workers. The photograph illustrates very well the geographical problems faced and conquered by 18th and 19th century engineers and workmen.

G.M. Jones

25. At about 2.30 p.m. on March 12, 1975, a breach was occasioned on the Brecon & Abergavenny canal about half a mile (0.8km) on the Pontypool side of Govilon and as a result half of the bed of the canal was washed away. Eventually ten miles (16km) of the waterway was closed and after inspection the consultant engineers, Sir William Halcrow and Partners, recommended lining lengths of the channel, the least expensive method being to lay concrete troughs where needful. This photograph shows a part of the work involved. The silt and original clay puddle was removed by Hymac excavators and a polythene membrane — to stop the stone from being ground into the mud — laid on top. After completion of the stone deposit, which is to provide drainage, the concrete can then be laid. By the end of 1978 nearly 3½ miles (5.6km) of channel was finished at an estimated cost of £483,000, largely under a 'Job Creation' scheme, with £80,000 or so being expended by the British Waterways Board to actually repair the breach.

26.   There is a scheme in hand to restore the Huddersfield Narrow canal to navigation but, wisely, the society concerned are concentrating on certain lengths which are in reasonable condition.   This photograph of 1975 is included to show not only the problems they face but also how, on a waterway which is nothing more or less than two staircases on either side of a tunnel, water control, with low maintenance costs, is best effected. This lock has been infilled with mass concrete and is bereft of gates.

27. Even more surprisingly there are plans to restore the Somerset Coal Canal. While many artifacts are almost indestructable, even with modern machines this seems a difficult task. Combe Hay Locks, 1967.

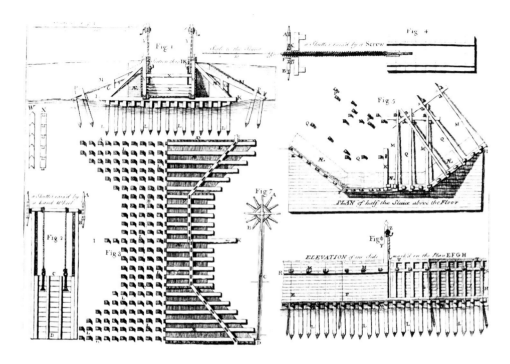

28. A watergate, or flash lock, for use in the navigation of small rivers, as detailed in 1763.   The main problem with this type of mechanism is that a 'small river' can become a raging torrent in a very short space of time, and it would be a brave man who ventured out when the whole arrangement was shaking like a jelly to wind the 'shutter' in order to let the water escape.   The inherent weakness of wooden locks — especially as no really good preservations were then available — was their proclivity to rot not so much underground but just above with the embedded stumps remaining sound.   This made replacement of the struts 'M' and 'N' on figure 1 (necessary every decade if they were to hold the sides in alignment) twice as hazardous.   The use of piles and a planked floor underneath the gate is interesting as this pattern still remains under superimposed brick floors of some early river locks.

29.   Medley or Binsey weir on the Thames was certainly photographed after 1865 for the iron bridge in the background was not built until then.   This bridge was, in effect, a changeline bridge for here the towpath swung over from side to side; prior to this the practice at low water was for the barge-horse to wade across, otherwise a 2½ mile (4km) trudge up one side of the river to the nearest bridge and back again down the other was required for it to be rejoined to the barge.   The weir itself is recorded as being in existence in the 12th century, although the flash lock was not installed until 1793.   By 1883 this weir was described as having contributed to the 'wretched' state of the river above; not the least problem for the bargees was that 'flashes' were only allowed on two days a week as the mills had to have priority.

Oxfordshire County Library

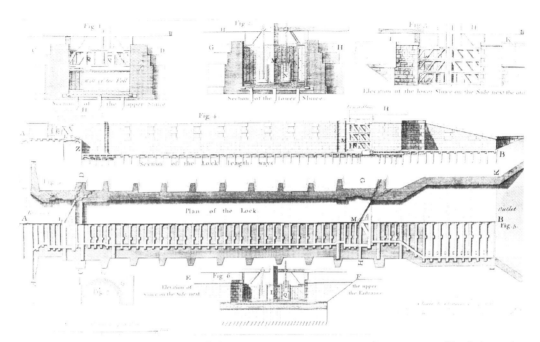

30.   A 1763 plan for a pound lock, which in many respects represents the pattern utilized throughout the canal system.   Piling and wooden sheeting as a bottom to a lock ceased to be very popular by about 1780 when brick, or occasionally stone, was substituted.   The 'wall of the fall' (Fig.1) was almost invariably brick with a wooden main-cill onto which a further clap-cill was (and is) spiked.   Paddles and their starts have tended over the years to migrate to the lock sides; particularly at the top end, partly as handling is safer, but also in times of poor maintenance to reduce the leakage occasioned by the weight of water penned back. On Midland canals, where both gate and ground paddles were still in situ during the twenty years after the 1939-45 war gate paddles were blocked off, ostensibly to reduce maintenance costs while ignoring the fact that lock filling time is greatly increased.   This shortsighted 'accountants' decision drove almost the final nail into the coffin of canal carriers as to them time equalled the difference between a trading profit and loss.

31. An original and rather primitive lock on the 'Old Union' — the Leicestershire & Northamptonshire canal — in reality a canalisation of the River Soar. This particular lock, Swans Mill, and its neighbour, Castle, were demolished sometime between 1885 and 1888 when the Leicester Corporation lowered, widened and straightened the waterway through the city to relieve the local flooding problem. The old line ran across the local football ground, while Freeman's Meadow (locally 'New') lock, No.41, was built as a substitute. The lock-keeper in the photograph is Joseph Nokes, together with his wife Matilda and some of their family. The balance beam and rickety paddle gearing betray the poor financial state of this waterway.

L. Hales

32. The Shrewsbury canal, although initially profitable for its proprietors, was nevertheless an uneasy fusion of a tub- and narrow-boat canal, which eventually stultified trade. In 1799 the local newspaper complained that the waterway, by its monopoly of trade, had raised the price of coal, although during this period inflation was so bad boots had, by 1800, risen in price from 20p (in 1795) to 28p and coal generally from £1.43 (in 1790) to £2.15 a ton. The route was from Castle Foregate Basin in Shrewsbury to Longdon, some 12 miles (19km) all at one level, then a series of locks raised it 79ft (24m) in the next 4¼ miles (7.2km) to Wombridge where there was an inclined plane, after which it linked up with the Donnington Wood canal a mile or so further on. The inclined plane was built to take 8-ton tub-boats 20ft (6m) x 6ft 6in (1.98m) which were in use on neighbouring waterways. The locks and bridges were, therefore, designed only to accommodate craft of this beam and when narrow-boats came into use these were necessarily long and thin to fit the 82ft (25m) x 6ft 7in (1.99m) locks, which was to their detriment when eventually a connection was made with the branch of the Birmingham & Liverpool Junction (now Shropshire Union Main Line) canal in 1835, whose locks were a nominal 70ft (21.3m) x 7ft (21.1m). As this junction opened up a more direct route to the midland/western markets, plans were advanced to convert the locks and bridges to the wider beam but for financial reasons only two locks and the bridges between Shrewsbury and Wappenshall were so altered. In this photograph, taken in the 1950s, twenty or so years after traffic ceased, the chain from the winding gear on the right to the gate has been removed, the other goes to a counterweight which operated in a well covered by the bramble bush on the left.

L.A. Edwards

44

33.   Once known locally as 'Big Wheel', Bran or Brandon Staunch was photographed over seventy years ago when the Little Ouse or Brandon River was navigable by Fen lighters from Thetford to its junction with the Ouse at Brandon Creek.   Eight of these navigation weirs were in existence on a river which had been continually improved since, at least, 1670.   It was also the scene and indirectly the cause of many floods, not least when the landowners high-up fearing the waters would back up to their relatively prosperous ground sent their men to blow the banks, irregardless of whether or not the Fenmen scratching a living lower down were drowned or their clay-lump cottages destroyed.   Navigation, other than with a dinghy, is now only possible below Brandon for 13 miles (21km) out of the earlier 22 (35km) due to fixed sluices having replaced these watergates.

45

34. A standard narrow lock with a top end gate paddle lifted. Installed originally to speed the filling of a lock, these are now almost extinct as the waters' impact on light pressure craft sends them clattering to the other end of the lock and damage can ensue.

35. Widmead Lock on the Kennet & Avon canal navigation was photographed before restoration and while an extremely sad sight is, nevertheless, an excellent example of a turf-sided lock. The main reason for using this type of construction can only have been economy, as they were tediously slow to fill and empty due to absorption of water by the boskage. Until the addition of the guards (made from redundant rail) there was always the problem, when the lock was full, of knowing exactly where the lock-cut was, as it was not always in the dead centre. In times of flood the chamber had a greater capacity to hold water but conversely the gates and their quoins were prone to movement.

R. Liddiard

47

36. Glamorganshire canal, Abercynon, c.1880.   Virtually all southern Welsh canals were forced to climb higher in a shorter distance than their English equivalents to get near the iron-works and collieries that were to be their lifeblood.   Locks were narrow and the track forced to find its way wherever it could, jostling for space with the roads and rivers.   Typically, the Glamorganshire incorporated 51 locks in 25½ miles (41 km), rising around 543 ft (166 m).   Note that the windlass appears to be fixed (this practice, according to memories, only being discontinued at the very end of the canals' life), and that top-cills or lintels are in use to hold the gates square; possibly due to distortion from subsidence which led to the closure of this section on 6th December 1889.   By 1910 it was derelict.   To the right is the necessary adjunct to any Welsh town or village, the chapel — in this case Calfaria Welsh Baptist.

Western Mail

37. The Caledonian canal, probably the most spectacular of Telford's works, is shown here c. 1900 at Fort Augustus. Lock Ness in the background completes a typical view of this navigation which is, in effect, a series of artificial and natural cuts. Completed in 1822, the 60 miles (97km) and 29 locks of this waterway were partly built with Government aid, taking in all 19 years for completion. Prior to the modern electromechanical installations the enormous, four armed, capstans were absolutely vital to open the gates. Due to the weight involved it was obviously impossible to fit orthodox balance beams if they were, as their name suggests, to counter-balance the drag of the wood and ironwork, and these capstans were substituted. The paddler, possibly the *Gondolier*, was one of a number heavily used in summer by sightseeing parties between Inverness and Banavie, indeed by 1905 the toll-income from such vessels represented 20 per cent of the total.

38.) Hartford Lock and its weir, River Weaver, was first built in timber sometime during 1731/1732, and was
39.) one of ten or eleven installed around this time, to increase trade in coal (up) and salt (down) with smaller quantities of clay and 'merchants goods' also being catered for.   These improvements allowed craft of 35+ tons to move at most times of the year.   Between 1778 and 1800 trade had increased to a level where new, permanent, locks could be justifiably installed, the tonnage (still mainly coal and salt) having trebled over the 30 years between 1759 and 1789.   One major problem on the waterway was that although a bow-hauling (man-haulage) towpath was built in the 1730s it was not until 60 years later that horse-towing became possible,

(38) Waterways Museum, Stoke Bruerne

50

but even with the introduction of steam flats both systems remained in use costing, in the 1850s, for the round trip Northwich-Weston Point, £1 for a horse and man or £1.50 for six men. Trade was by then so extensive that a number of locks were duplicated in the 1860s, although this was only a short-term measure, Hartford locks finally being eliminated in 1891. (38) was taken during the mid-1180s and (39) in 1978. The only common factors shown in both photographs are the round of the lock wall and the railway viaduct discernable in the distance.

(39) M. Newton, Northwich Rowing Club

40. Melange at Bristol. Netham lock in 1965. Virtually every item and building in the photograph is of a period.   This lock and part of the Avon navigation was opened in 1727 and subsequently incorporated in the Kennet & Avon canal navigation.   Within the last few years the developers heavy hand has struck and the background, at least, has changed beyond recognition.   It will be noted that visible gates are all open, the lock is so built that when levels permit – the river being tidal – boats can work straight through.

41. Detail of paddle gearing, a symphony in iron, stone and wood.

53

42. The first lock at Knostrop was built by 1700, as a part of the Aire navigation but the line of the navigation was always plagued by the presence of mills and its extremely shallow draught; with only 2ft 6in (0.76m) over the lock sills in summer craft tonnage was small.   William Jessop, under the direction of John Smeaton, was called in in 1772 to prepare plans for the modernisation of the rivers Aire and Calder; although in 1774, during its passage through Parliament, his plan for the new Knostrop Cut incorporating two locks was truncated to have only one in order to protect the water supply to Thwaite Mill.   This new cut was completed by 1779 and within a year 2,200 boats had passed through the lock.   Again in 1823 traffic having justified a larger lock at Knostrop this was built together with a flood-lock.   During the early 1860s, keeping abreast of demand, W.H. Bartholomew, engineer to the Aire & Calder navigation, drew up plans for a further re-building of the locks from Goole to Castleford (completed by 1867) and to Wakefield and Leeds 1869 and 1873 respectively thus enabling steam barges with a capacity of 150-200 tons to work throughout.   Seen here around 1910 Knostrop can now, as a result of further works, accommodate craft 180ft (54.9m) x 18ft 6in (5.6m) x 10ft (3m) draught, carrying 500 tons; it is almost unrecognisable compared with this view.

P.L. Smith

43.   Industrial past.   A number of the components of this lock, Wightwick, Staffordshire & Worcestershire canal, are in excess of two hundred years old.   The gate gearing is one of the few remaining examples, for as gates are renewed this ironwork is no longer replaced, mainly on the grounds of economy but also as some modern boat owners appear to misunderstand their operation and they flood the fore-ends of their boats. The ground paddle-start in the left background is of the original pattern.   The blue brick copings are non-original but were certainly put in place prior to the first world war; some bearing the date '1894'.   The hand rail between the gearing shows many impacts from boats fore-ends.

44.　Midlands industrial lock at Walsall 1972 typifies the waterways of this area.　The bridge of a standard pattern is a relatively late example replacing one damaged by subsidence.　The handrail of the top gate is kinked where some boat failed to check its way in time although the gate paddle whose spindle is immediately below the handrail is still in situ.　The old stable block-cum-boatman's hovel, latterly a maintenance workman's shed, is　derelict　and thanks to both vandals and weather is being de-roofed.　From its smell and appearance its last service was as a lavatory and no doubt it will disappear shortly.　The bottom end gate betrays its age for rope wear is not only visible on the handrail but also on the gearing and balance beam.　This was caused as the horse took the strain of the boat at an angle on entering or leaving the lock — this animal was motor and brake simultaneously — and the rope rubbed along the wood or iron.　The friction must surely have been an unnecessary extra strain on the animal, but such bad design — at least in some part due to lack of forethought — was common.　It could, to some extent and where circumstances permitted, be mitigated by the use of a longer line from boat to horse although this pre-supposed such an item was available.　Too many of the day boats which used the Birmingham Canal Navigations were very scantily equipped due to thieving by both boatmen and the public.

45. The Bridgwater & Taunton canal possesses more odd minutae in its fifteen and a quarter miles (24.5m) than many others do in double that length.   Shown here is Standard Lock at the top end. Ground paddles are utilised, the chain of the counterweight runs over the pulley to the paddle, this with the reduction gear fitted makes operation relatively easy.   The non-automatic safety catch is visible on the right hand side of the pinion.

46.   Not all waterways put their monograms in the same places, some were meticulous in marking tools and little else, others mile-posts or paddle gearing, but only a few bothered with items like this gate anchor.   This, in any event, could be a waste of time as letters cast proud will more often than not have been worn away over the 150 or 200 years a waterway has been in use.   This particular set were depressed into the sandstone and hence protected to some extent but even so it was necessary to pick out the lettering for photographic purposes.   Seen here in 1972, Worcester & Birmingham Canal Company breaks the cipher!

47.   Many views of Bingley 3- and 5-rise (staircase) locks are published, but this is a gem.   Believed to date back to just prior to World War I, the period atmosphere has been caught by the photographer.   It is known that the gentleman in the foreground wearing a bowler hat was Alfred Turner, the then carpenter on the Yorkshire side of the Leeds & Liverpool canal.   The tool he is holding was an adze, itself symbolic of his position.   This may be seen in use today for trimming gates and particularly when old-type paddles have to be fitted or faced to match the framing of the paddle-hole.   Latterly though this tool is falling into disuse as both gates and paddles are being fitted with strips of artificial material which absorb any irregularities and wear.   The bowler hat served well in lieu of today's protective headgear for it could absorb the impact of a brick without undue damage.

48.   This photograph taken some time in the 1920s, of maintenance work in progress on the Sheffield &
South Yorkshire New Junction canal at Sykehouse is mainly of interest in that there is a slab of newly dressed
stone immediately in the foreground; although its purpose is in doubt it has the appearance of being an
anchor stone normally used to carry the weight of the gates.   The overflow culvert behind has also been
broken open showing its construction.   The New Junction canal was not opened until 1905, having been
built under the Superintendence of William H. Bartholomew, although he had officially retired ten years
previously!

P.L. Smith

49.   This photograph poses a slight mystery as there is some uncertainty both as to location and the exact date, although Sykehouses lock on the New Junction canal around 1910 has been suggested.   The men's actions, however, are clear beyond doubt.   Until mechanical plant was introduced in the 1920s locks were cleared of debris by hand, and where heavy or tidal traffic was involved this might be necessary every two or three years.   The operation simplicty itself, either the mud was shovelled to a staging halfway up the side of the lock or a manual or steam crane was utilised to lift either wheelbarrows or dustbins which the men standing within the chamber filled with muck.   Although this style of working is occasionally reverted to even now modern canalmen have two advantages, 'hard hats' (safety helmets) are compulsory and rubber boots, rather than the leather of these men, are worn; nonetheless, it is still a particularly filthy and smelly job.   The wheelbarrows came in two sizes, small for navvies and large for dredgers, and were made in the Company's workshops.   The wedged beams running horizontally across the chamber are lock-hangers which, suspended by chains from above, normally carry a staging for bricklayers or masons to work from.

P.L. Smith

61

50.   The job of water scooping, necessary to clear the bottom of a lock prior to bricklayers work, was always given to a new or disgruntled labourer.   Such work quickly sorted the sheep from the goats.

J.K. Ebblewhite

51.   The Basingstoke canal was opened in 1796 and finally fell into disuse after the second world war. Restoration works are proceeding but not under the eye of the British Waterways Board, for this was one of the very few waterways neither railway owned nor nationalised.   The county councils of Surrey and Hampshire instead held the overriding responsibility with Surrey & Hants Canal Society volunteers doing the donkey-work.   Due to a lack of heavy lifting plant the practice is to cut the gates up in situ using the chainsaw on the lockside above the quoin.   The figures on the left and right are cutting out, replacing and repointing rotten brickwork.   More mud is in evidence than on a British Waterways Board controlled stoppage but less safety helmets.   Top end, Lock 17, 1978.

A. Lucas

53.) Occasional meteors pass through the canal firmament and one of these was the American, Robert
54.) Fulton, whose fertile brain envisioned the use of steam canal boats, back pumping of water by steam engines, mechanical diggers and the use of inclined planes and lifts as substitutes for locks where the geography of the land precluded adequate water supplies. He also tried submersible craft. The underlying theme of most of his plans for waterways was to use small 'tub' boats, with a capacity of 3 to 5 tons, which would move

along a canal to the nearest surmountable hill then via a lift or plane rise sharply to the next height and so on, thus obviating locks and water shortages. Some planes were to be counterbalanced (ascending boats by those descending), others single boat operated by a 'bucket-in-a-well' principle with the weight of water in the bucket balancing the boat whether empty or full. Burnt out from striving to press his plans he died aged 50 in 1815, nineteen years after the publication of these drawings.

52. Cast iron beauty. A portion of Kings Norton Guillotine Lock which was built to measure the water used between the Worcester & Birmingham and Stratford canals. The lock itself is set against a rather dreary backdrop and particularly disappointing to visitors since the bridge-house was demolished. For all that this gaunt disused frame sits well against the tracery of branches. January, 1966.

55. Pure nostalgia. In the far off days when a lock-keeper was responsible for one lock, or just a handful, he showed his pride. Not only were the locks painted but gardens were trim, and adjacent to most the name of the lock (or sometimes just its number) was displayed. The late Tom Hughes, for many years an employee on the Worcester & Birmingham canal, stubbornly kept to the old standards long after he retired and 'his' nameboard is seen here, painted in red and gold, in 1976. Following his death and the subsequent demolition of the lockhouse this nameplate was removed before vandals could strike.

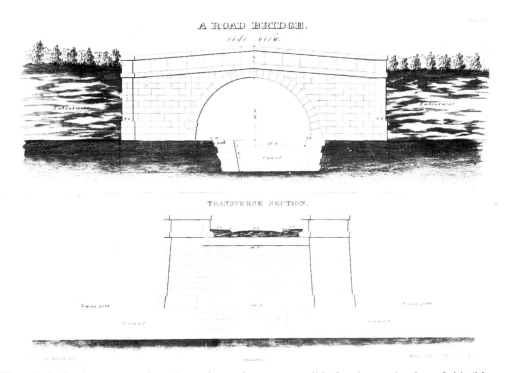

A ROAD BRIDGE.
side view.

TRANSVERSE SECTION.

56.   William Strickland appears to have been the engineer responsible for the production of this 'blue-print', reproduced in a book published in 1838.   It is intended to represent a bridge on the Birmingham & Liverpool Junction (now the main line of the Shropshire Union canal network) which was built between its terminals of Autherley and Nantwich under the guidance of both Thomas Telford and, following Telford's death, William Cubitt.   This was the last of Telford's works, intended to rival (or extinguish) the plans for a new-fangled railroad.   For all the pressures that were put upon Thomas Telford to cut corners and thus speed up the works by the proprietors, who foresaw financial problems looming, he flatly refused to allow standards to fall; the majority of these bridges are still standing nearly a century and a half later.

57. Melton Mowbray Navigation. This bridge, photographed in 1966, was built at the time the River Wreake was canalised and shows how the invert or bottom is almost a mirror image of the arch. As this is only a bypass to the old lock-pound and river course it was unlikely to carry a vast quantity of water, and the only visible damage to the brickwork appears to have been caused by frost.

58.   A bridge undergoing demolition.   The arch has already been taken down by an excavator thus re-opening the canal for traffic and the remainder of the brickwork can then be dealt with by maintenance men as it becomes possible.   This photograph, taken in the mid-1960s shows the construction of a common accommodation bridge.   The top layer of rubble in the roadway should be ignored, the standard nineteenth century finish was either small stone or gravel.   Each brick measures, roughly, 9" x 4" (23 x 10cm), the thickness of the parapet and arching is, therefore, about 15" (38cm).

B. Holding

59. When a landowner was requested to allow part of his land to be used in order that a canal might be built he could, if influential enough, demand that the canal company make any structure an amenity instead of what he considered to be an eyesore. The company were not over-enthusiastic as the cost of a bridge like this, Avenue Bridge No.10 on the Shropshire Union (ex-Birmingham & Liverpool Junction) canal was very much greater than that of an orthodox structure, and they could contest the suggestion to as great a degree as was possible. Often these estates were 'new', having been obtained from the profits of mills or ironworks; these entrepreneurs were harder to deal with than the real gentry. This bridge, however, leads to Chillington Hall, home of the Giffard family since the 12th century.

60.　　　The presence of pebbles or other foreign materials in brickwork almost inevitably leads to moisture entering and then, in winter, freezing, whereupon the bricks delaminate and end up looking like this. In this particular case no structural damage was done to the bridge but should the lower courses be so affected then eventually demolition will be necessary. A common, in fact monotonously regular, complaint laid against contractors by engineers was the appallingly low standard of their brickwork but as bricks were quite often supplied by the canal company to the hapless contractor he had no choice but to do the best he could. With handmade bricks there were too many weak links in the chain from the puddler whose feet missed the pebbles to the stoker who failed to keep an even temperature in the kiln; these in this photograph, made at a local brickyard, were both pebbly and 'green'.

61.   Canals offered the opportunity for the iron trade to expand by giving the blast furnaces easy access to supplies of their basic requirements — ore, limestone and coal.   Conversely as they produced more castings canal companies offered them cheap rates for their transportation and were in turn offered discounts on items they required.   The canal companies were only too pleased to accept these and the cut-throat competition between ironworks ensured keen pricing, to a level where for a time even the prime cost of bridges like this was far lower than building in brick.   Photographed at Ogley Junction where the Anglesey Branch (opened 1850) left the Wyrley & Essington canal line to the Coventry canal (opened 1797, closed 1954).   The ribs of this bridge having been exposed by neglect, the original ash covering having eroded away.   However at some time mining has caused subsidence and movement of the arch, and the rigidity of cast iron did not allow the flexing that is found in a brick bridge, therefore reinforcing straps have been riveted to the arch. Apart from the obvious function of lightening the weight of the bridge on the foundations without loss of strength there was no obvious reason by an ironmaster and canal engineer, both matter-of-fact men, should between them have created beauty, but by any standard it is apparent.

62. The changing face of waterways. The building on the right was once the Kings Norton Paper Mills where coal was shovelled from boats through apertures newly bricked up in the wall — it is claimed a competent boatman and his mate would shovel out twenty tons in three hours. When this photograph was taken, 1975, the premises had been taken over by a firm of car distributors who had their main 'pen' on the left hand side of the canal and built this bridge to get vehicles there. It cannot be said to add to the visual amenities of the area. The row of trees marks the course of the river Rea, the culvert of which, under the canal, is too often blocked by the detritus of our civilisation — anything from drums of hydrochloric acid via mattresses to aerosol cans, all of which have to be burnt, a most unpleasant job for the maintenance men involved. The vicinity is now landscaped as part of the Patrick Motor Museum.

63.   It has been claimed, with some justification that canals by their extensive usage of tramroads as feeders led the way to the development of railways.   Certainly when the railway network was at its peak the effect on waterways was to change not only their trading results but their entire physical appearance. As railways are closed the relics eventually dwindle and to a passing boatman the line might never have been. The Great Central Railway had a short life but ultra-modern in its' outlook no attempt was made to conceal its being. En route to London it crossed and re-crossed the Leicester arm of the Grand Union canal and particularly within the city of Leicester provided a piquant contrast between the latest locomotives hauling fitted freight or passenger trains and elderly motorboats hauling butties.   Here A3 class Pacific 60106 *Flying Fox* with the full majesty of a steam locomotive on display hauls the South Yorkshireman away from Leicester.

C.P. Walker

DEBDALE LOCK COOLEY

64.   A rather unusual view of Debdale Bridge and Lock, on the Staffordshire & Worcestershire canal, taken around the turn of the century.   The sole access to a road from the cottage was (and is) via the towpath or the bridge.   In the days before piped water when the drought caused his well to dry up, the lock-keeper would put a container on a downhill boat, the full one being brought back by the next uphill boat.   The apparent hardship of this procedure was eased by there being a daily average of 20 boats as late as 1932. The bridge is unusual, if not unique, but the little cast iron lock tail bridge behind, which is split in two to allow the boat's line to pass, is one of four on the waterway.   The horse is re-fueling ready for the long haul.

Birmingham Public Libraries

65. The tank, or Barton Aqueduct, which carries the Bridgewater canal over the Manchester Ship canal. When this latter was being built it was necessary to demolish Brindley's old structure and as a replacement which would give sufficient headroom Mr. (later Sir) E. Leader Williams settled for this design, whereby the tank is swung full of water. It was opened on 21st August, 1893, after being delayed by a bank failure. The engraving is based on a drawing of the 1900s when barges, mainly horse-drawn were so common as not to justify comment for it was this traffic that originally caused a change of plan from the original proposal for a high level aqueduct connected by 'Anderton-type' lifts; a proposal rejected because the delays would be too great "in view of the traffic".   Hydraulically powered, the moving span is 71.6m (235ft) long and weighs, including water, 1,450 tons.

J.K. Ebblewhite

66. Canal bridges, and particularly those of Thomas Telford, have an unselfconscious charm. Whether built from brick or stone they have the beauty of functional line allied to an unerring sense of perspective.

67. The greatest 'Wonder of the Waterways'. Standing 115.8m (126ft 8in) "from the surface of the flat rock on the south side of the river Dee" to the top of the trough, the first stone of the arches was laid in 1795 and the channel was opened for traffic six years later at a cost of £47,069. In all 307m (1007ft) in length, the 19 primary arches are of 13.7m span (45ft) each, and made from iron cast at Plas Kynaston by William Hazledine. The original plans by William Turner, approved by the principal engineer William Jessop, called for a massive three-arched masonry aqueduct and, indeed, contracts were placed on this basis in 1794. However, William Jessop, 18 months later recommended a volte-face by proposing the use of iron with seven arches of 15.2m (50ft) each, the remainder of the crossing of the Dee to be by way of earthen embankments. Jessop, resident at Newark-on-Trent was one of four partners, together with Benjamin Outram, Francis Beresford and John Wright, in the Butterley Ironworks and his proposal, backed as it was with experience and having behind it the enthusiasm of Thomas Telford, was favourably received. Bearing in mind its dimensions, it was relatively quickly finished and the quality of workmanship was such that it is substantially the same aqueduct we can cross over or view today. The engraving is dated 1811.

79

Could'nt we put a lock in, Mr. Telford?

68.   With the various changes in plan it is a miracle that this did not happen during the building of Pont-cysyllte.   Telford however, chose his contractors well — had Pinkerton or the Dadfords been either engineers or contractors no doubt the aqueduct would have collapsed long since.

J.K. Ebblewhite

69. By way of contrast a stone built aqueduct, designed by Sir John Rennie, carries the Lancaster canal over the River Lune, with little of the grace of Telford work.

Lancaster Guardian

70/71/72. In 1961 work was undertaken on the Lancaster canal to replace Bulk Road aqueduct — a typical structure of John Rennie's design — with a new pre-stressed concrete trough as road widening to accommodate the new spur road connecting Lancaster with the M6 motorway was necessary.   As this meant bisecting the canal for over twelve months, a neat high level gantry was installed connecting with slipways at each end. Boats were manoevred onto a cradle and carriage, drawn out of the water up the slipway, trundled the 100 yards (91m) along the gantry and lowered at the other end via the other slipway.   In all within the twelve months nearly 300 boats had an airborne passge.

70. The original masonry acqueduct at Lancaster, opened 1796.   *Lancaster Guardian*

71. Seemingly dry docking facilities were made available.

Lancaster Guardian

72. En route.

Lancaster Guardian

71. The tunnel at Hardham on the Arun navigation, as depicted in 1868, a mere 79 years after its opening. This was a part of a very well thought out and thoroughly executed canalisation of a river, and although only 375 yards (343m) long, this tunnel represented quite an adventurous bit of engineering by the standards of the time and district.   As early as 1832 its condition had deteriorated for lack of maintenance and complaints arose due to the enforced stoppages of trade necessary while emergency repairs were carried out.   Matters were exacerbated by the necessity for boatmen to 'leg' or shaft their boats through, in a tunnel so short the omission of a towpath seems rather pennypinching.   The last trading boat passed through in 1889.

74.   Armitage is no more! Demolition taking place during 1971 — the original rock walls can be clearly seen as is (in the background) the steel re-inforcing which was inserted as a temporary expedient to retain the rock and give a reasonable, although restricted, passage for boats.   A new bridge now exists on the site.

British Waterways Board

75. When the Thames & Medway canal was converted into a railway in 1845 Higham tunnel was far too good to waste. Here a Stirling 4-4-0, built 1898, hauls her train from the ex-canal bore.

R.W. Kidner

76A.) During 1974/5 new tunnels were built over the Main Lines of the Birmingham Canal Navigations. Un-
76B.) like traditional canal tunnels these were not bored through an extant hill with the walls left rough hewn or brick lined, but instead were prefabricated concrete structures with the topsoil being added after. The purpose of both is to carry a new main road, thus relieving a historic monument – Telford's beautiful Galton Road bridge – of motor traffic. (76A) shows the old main line stanked off with the tunnel still a bare shell prior to the entry of water and with only the basic outline and towpath retaining wall in situ. (76B) the tunnel on the new main line about twelve months later. The strangest part of this artifact is that while Telford in his modernisation scheme put two towpaths along the canal the new tunnel only has one. The restricted cross-section has also ensured that wide beam craft will not now traverse Birmingham although such a scheme might have otherwise been feasible.

77. During the heyday of waterways — roughly the 75 years from 1760 — innumerable factories, foundries and mills built premises alongside the new canals not only to gain the advantage of quick, reliable and efficient transport but, upon payment of relatively small fees, they could draw water to feed their plant; quantities were not small: 90,000 litres (20,000 gallons) per day were needed at Huddersfield alone, and although most of this water was returned its continual supply was essential for the canal companies to be fully profitable. Now bedraggled, no doubt when John Hawthorn opened his canalside foundry it was an advertisement for his business.

A.J. Pierce

78.   An incredibly detailed steel engraving of Leeds City basin in 1829, based on a drawing by N. Whitlock. To obtain a good photograph of a similar scene today it is only necessary to have an expensive fully automatic camera, point and click.   This was initially an artist's impression, which, in itself, called for a tighter discipline than that of an oil-painter who can 'fudge' detail, and secondly called for strict interpretation by the engraver if accuracy was to be attained.   The stone bridge in the background was replaced in 1873, the chimneys show Leeds' industry, the hoist on the left is functional, the transom-sterned barge discharging barrels and crates is probably ex the Leeds & Liverpool canal but the Aire & Calder navigation barges on the right are bluff and tailored to fit the locks.   The whole scene is really alive.

Leeds Public Library

79.   By contrast a photograph taken from Leeds Bridge sometime about 1910 which shows the traffic then in use on the Aire & Calder navigation.   Quiescent, there are nevertheless eleven barges of various patterns including in the foreground a barge-master using the oldest way of moving an unpowered vessel.   The pole, shaft or quant would be about 20ft (6m) long and equipped with a shoulder pad.   The affinity of some of these barges with traditional Yorkshire keels is marked but the square chimneys are always a 'trade mark' of North Eastern vessels.   The lack of smoke from the chimney and movement of the wharves may well indicate this was a Sunday and — assuming the clock worked — we know the time.

Leeds Public Library

80.) The entrance to the Leeds & Liverpool canal in Leeds is seen in the middle 1920s and 1978. The 81.) building was a 'company' warehouse as can be seen by the lettering — Leeds and Liverpool Canal Company, General carriers — and was built in 1777, more or less at the same time as the opening of this length to Gargrave. The barge in the lock is a standard Leeds & Liverpool short-boat, 62ft x 14ft (18.9m x 4.3m)

(80) Leeds Public Library

92

and although these could work through to Liverpool, boats which were 10ft (3m) longer, carrying a greater tonnage, could work from Wigan to Liverpool — a part of this length having once represented the southern end of the Lancaster canal. This 'break-of-gauge' was eventually a hindrance to economic through-working. The barely discernable scene on the right was a boat-builders (a skeletal craft is on the stocks) and is now, alas, a car-park.

(81) A.J. Pierce

82.   In January 1972, this magnificent purpose-built warehouse complex was destroyed by fire, probably due to arson, but in any event it had long been neglected and left as a sitting target for vandals.   Their building had been recommended by Thomas Telford to cope with the increase of trade and although they were designed by him these warehouses, together with a new dock and other improvements, were eventually built by W.A. Provis as contractor under the new engineer William Cubitt in 1842/3 following the death of Telford in September 1834.   Described in September 1843 as 'a splendid and most ample range of warehouses, erected on arches over various branches of the canal', the last regular traffic from Ellesmere Port towards the Midlands, that of Thomas Clayton (Oldbury)Ltd., ceased in 1957-8 and thereafter the whole fell into disuse.

R. Bird

83.   The Pocklington canal was, in some ways, doomed almost before it was cut, serving as it did a rural population and terminating half-a-mile before, and well below, the town it was intended to receive its trade from, but nevertheless this warehouse at Canal Head was once busy enough.   This illustration of 1969 has been chosen as showing the state that a disused terminus can decline to when trade and boats are finished. Recently, with the co-operation of the British Waterways Board, volunteers from the Pocklington Canal Amenity Society have cleaned out the silt and overgrowth and changed the general appearance of the area to an unbelievable degree.

84.   One of the least known cuts must be that portrayed here sometime between 1900 and 1910.   It owes
its origins to a 1799 plan for a waterway to Croydon from the Thames at Wandsworth.   William Jessop,
called in to give his opinion, foresaw difficulties in water supply as it would have to come from the River
Wandle, and the 40 or so millers on that highly industrialised stream were not enamoured of the idea.   Jessop
suggested a tramroad for part of the way instead of a canal which materialised as the Surrey Iron Railway.
The connecting quarter of a mile (0.4km) canal from the Thames, this, MacMurray's, was opened on 9th
January 1802.   The tramroad was sold to the London, Brighton & South Coast Railway in 1839, but supplies
of coal to the Gas Works and the Ram Brewery kept the canal in business until the end of the first world war
when it was stanked off and gradually infilled.

M. Denney

85.   Moira, the one time terminus of the Ashby de la Zouch canal ceased to receive boats in 1944 when the length Moira/Donisthorpe was closed.   This illustration of 'The Furnace' at Moira cannot be dated accurately but probably goes back 100 years or so.   'The Furnace' was built by the local mine owners towards the end of the eighteenth century as a co-operative venture to provide castings for their industry, items produced varying from parts for winding engines to domestic grates.   'The Furnace' consisted of three separate buildings and although supplies of basic commodities required were easy to come by — limestone by tramroad from Ticknall and Cloud Hill, coal from adjacent collieries and iron ore by boat — its working life was only about 20 years, and from around 1820 it was used for domestic occupation.   The blast furnace (extant today) is to the right of the house.

T. Henshaw

86.   A fascinating juxaposition of canal engineering elements at Wrenbury on the Welsh branch of the Shropshire Union canal network.   The drawbridge is a slightly updated version of Thomas Telford's original design; counter-balanced, operation is by means of a pull on the chain to the nearest arm (tied down to stop slatting and banging), overrunning is stopped by means of the angled post on the far base, while the stone walling and ironwork are original.   For many years Wrenbury Mill was a mainstay of canal traffic and it is apposite that in this twenty year old photograph the stern of a traditional butty, or unpowered cargo boat, should be visible.

P.L. Smith

87.   Pensnett rail/canal interchange which provided a useful outlet not only for the L & NWR (as lessees of the Birmingham Canal Navigation) but also for the local collieries.   For both parties it obviated the expense of laying new track, purchasing land and, in a highly manually-intensive trade, employing labour.   The idea and its execution were simple.   Given that there were 159 miles of the BCN (a rather greater mileage of navigable waterways than Venice) with virtually every mile lined with factories, mainly having their own private arms, and that virtually all these factories used and required coal for some part of their business, it was infinitely preferable to use any track available rather than build new.   Various extant basins were converted as in this photograph, or new ones built, all with high level rail tracks and adequate laybyes for the boats.   Interestingly, even at this date, c.1920, the crane used for transferring wagons appears to be disused — but it was usual for wagon traversers (even plain sleepers where the trucks were joggled across by pinch bars) to be in use, thus reducing shunting.

Dudley Public Libraries

88. A purpose built engineering artifact at Moira on the Ashby-de-la-Zouch canal, photographed during or just after the first world war. This scene represents all that is now lost on waterways, for not only has this stretch of canal totally disappeared — due to subsidence problems caused by collieries — but so have the boats, while steam engines and private owner coal waggons have to be tracked down in their lairs instead of being commonplace.

Reservoir Colliery was formally opened on 26th September, 1852, and for some time a gantry and drop hoist enabled boats to be loaded directly from the pit box but the rebuilding of 1913 reintroduced this somewhat retrograde method of transhipment. Six main sizes of coal were offered from "Hand-picked" to slack, and the boat types on show are nearly as varied with the cabin-boats hailing from Oxford, Coventry and Poles-worth.

89. Where it was uneconomic to extend a canal, or where the physical nature of the land made constant water supplies dubious, a horse-drawn tramway was commonly substituted. Derby Canal c.1880.

90. Historic scenery.   Perhaps because of the camera angle this hoist appears to be on the move but the motor-barge *Lyric* has completed discharging her cargo of silica sand at a Knottingley glass works on the Aire & Calder navigation in 1970.   This is one of the few wateways which has kept pace with modern demand. and the British Waterways Board's Commercial Manager is quick to seize on any traffics offered, however unorthodox.

P.L. Smith

91. Church Minshull, Middlewich or Wardle Branch, Shropshire Union canal is remote and divorced from the village, which in any event only had a population of 282 in 1931. The cottage at rear was, in 1975, semi-derelict, having been on offer for leasing from the British Waterways Board as long ago as the mid-1950s. The stable block held some lengthmen's bits and bobs, but has long forgotten the smell and sound of horses. The approximate date of these buildings was, for once, easily ascertained for the bricks were made locally and boated from Brickyard Bridge, No. 6, about half-a-mile (0.8km) or so away. This brickyard, as far as can be established, only produced this particular pattern of brick between 1831 and 1839. The piling is a particularly good example of the modern galvanised convoluted design, smartly driven and neatly finished.

92.   When the Birmingham Canal Navigations main line was rebuilt by Telford considerable thought was given to the collection of tolls having in mind the two essentials of speed and accuracy.   These functionally beautiful toll-houses were built near junctions and by virtue of their design gave excellent visibility for the toll-collector and by working south-bound boats through one side and north-bound through the other delays were minimised.   A bar was dropped across, thus halting the boat, the tonnage was read off on gauging sticks, a 'chit' or payment tendered and the boat was free to go with only a few minutes detention.   For many years traffic justified manning these on a twenty-four hour basis; with two keepers (later one) on duty at all times. This particular building was situated near Bromford Bridge, Spon Lane.   The New Line coming from Tipton continues to the right, while the left hand line leads to the foot of the three Spon Lane locks, which gave access to the Engine Branch as well as innumerable factories along this older route.   Incidentally, Spon Lane locks themselves are the oldest working locks on the whole of the BCN.   The two iron accommodation bridges are an interesting contrast in styles, but the brick bridge just visible alongside the toll-office carried the towpath over a factory arm.   The toll-office was photographed in 1955; being demolished a few years later.

Dudley Public Library

104

93.   Gailey lock, Staffordshire & Worcestershire canal, has one detail in common with six of the locks on the Thames & Severn canal, in that the lockhouse is round.   It is a matter of contention precisely why they were so built, in theory visibility is improved and yet the cost of building (normally a matter of the greatest importance to canal companies) is far higher.   Photographed in 1976 with a suitable — and rare — carrying boat neatly posed!

M. Black

94. An aspect of canal engineering which, too often, is overlooked. Pannell's Yard for all its rather temporary appearance was one of the first to be built on the river Welland when, at the request of shipmasters, John Pannell obtained permission to lay in a slipway as long ago as 1837. The 'billy-boy' Laurel is seen under repair sometime in the 1870s; the yard saw another half-century of shipwork. The building behind the yard workshop is believed to have been a public house, the object in front is one of a pair of vertical windlasses used to drag boats up the slipway.

Gentlemen's Society, Spalding

*" Now the Government's spending
five million quid to save the
canals, this'll be our last chance of
dumping all this old rubbish."*
Courtesy Manchester Evening News

95.   Rubbish dumping on waterways has gone on now for as long as they have existed — one imagines some Roman maintenance man on the Caer Dyke complaining bitterly about "lumps of old bronze laying about"! — in this case it was fortunate, as such debris has allowed archaeologists to date the canal, but the cartoon is all too apposite; neither sentiment nor the law can stop midnight visitations.

96.   The earliest dredging on canals was carried out manually when a stretch of waterway would be closed and the mud, bricks, rubble, iron and other waste shovelled out.   The first mobile unit was the spoon dredger which could not handle more than 20 tons a day.   Steam brought a vast improvement to this figure and a dredger of the type shown here could, theoretically, discharge 400 tons in a working period.   This, though, carried two penalties, a minimum of eight men as crew and its very success acted as a disincentive to produce anything better, machines of this pattern remaining in use until the 1960s when wages were far higher. Working conditions, for stokers and mud scrapers alike, were bad and the exposed machinery hazardous; the trunking protects the extractor but not the drive belts.   The Aire & Calder maintenance gang are at work on the Selby canal, c.1927.

P.L. Smith

108

97. The changing fortunes of waterway boats is well depicted here at Stoke Prior, Worcester & Birmingham canal, 1968. From left to right an iron day boat, formerly used on the Coventry canal for the carriage of coal, slack and ashes, has the basic frames for a cabin in situ; the *Mole* dredger, now rebuilt, is in her original form of 1956; the boat with its cabin almost complete is the onetime icebreaker *Scott*, with a modified stern but the original bows and hulls, and the last on the right is an ex-Potteries 'Fly' (Express Goods) boat of 1911, with a larch-built hull which had become (commercially) life-expired. The background shows a part of the salt works, themselves now demolished.

98. This strange looking, but extremely efficient, craft is built by the Liverpool Water Witch Engineering Company Limited and used by the British Waterways Board for a number of purposes. The primary objective is the removal of floating debris from the canal, material that can range from polystyrene slabs to barely floating oil-drums but such is its versatility that floating weed can be cleared from the channel thus obviating the necessity to spray on chemicals; this latter operation having quite rightly raised great oppostion not only from environmental pressure groups but even canalside housewives who feed the waterfowl and do not like them being driven away. *Waterways Witch 3* is seen on the Leeds & Liverpool canal in 1977.

British Waterways Board

99.   When dredging has been carried out the resulting slurry, a combination of eroded soil, coal, beer bottles, prams and other junk, must be disposed of.   Vital in the days of commercial boats here is Braunston (Grand Union) Mud Tip No.5, 10th May, 1911.

Waterways Museum

100. Dredging — the clearance of mud, rubbish, scrap and other obstructions from the channel — is of vital importance. When canals were first built, despite the fact, or more probably because of it, that boats were of greater draft, there were surprisingly few complaints. The earliest method used was to close a section of waterway and then use "a vast multitude of labourers" to shovel or throw everything out. In 1814-15 a machine was developed "to clear Mud & Filth out of the Canal without drawing out the water" but it was not until the 1850s that steam dredgers were normally in use. These were, alas, slow, expensive to operate and unwieldy, so for lock clearance the old manual method, throwing from the bottom, first to staging and then to the side was commonplace until a decade ago. The 'New Look' working, still restricted by access, is shown here in 1973.

101. The new generation of canal navvies often have resource to the methods of their predecessors. Here volunteers are clearing the chamber of Lock 15, Basingstoke canal, in 1978. The conditions are atrocious although as most canal volunteers only work on site at odd weekends they can regard the whole operation with great humour; unlike the dour expressions normally seen on the faces of the British Waterways Board's workmen who have five days of shovelling to face each week!

A. Lucas

102. The end of a waterway. This illustration of 1903 shows a steam driven power jig driving piles into the bed of the Kensington canal during the building of Lots Road Power Station (1902-1905) which was to be used in conjunction with the forthcoming electrification of the District Railway. The Kensington, once a proud barge-carrying canal, ran 1 3/4 miles (2.8km) from north of what is now Cromwell Road to the Thames, adjacent to this scene. Opened 1828 it had (by 1978) been brutally truncated to a few hundred yards of barely navigable creek. The District Railway, now just another part of London's Underground System was, steam-hauled, opened between 1868 and 1871 and converted to electric power throughout by the end of 1905.

Illustrated London News

103. Bank reclamation works on the River Welland, Spalding, probably photographed in 1921/2. Roughly two dozen men employed on the work, which involved shifting thousands of tons of soil — no dredging having been undertaken for over 50 years this was long overdue! Some of the waste was used in the creation of Ayscoughes Gardens; the residue in private gardens.

Gentlemen's Society, Spalding

104. Piling by means of compressed air hammers is undeniably better than when 25.4kg (56 lb) sledge-hammers, not too affectionately nicknamed 'Monday', were in use. Incidentally, 'Tuesday' 12.7kg (28 lb) was just about capable of handling the job but anything lighter — 'Wednesday', 6.2kg (14 lb), 'Thursday', 3.1kg (7 lb), 'Friday', 1.6kg (3½lb) or the 'Saturday' "toffee-hammer" — hurt the wrists too much.

There are problems and discomforts attached to this relatively new, but already outmoded system. The weight of the pneumatic hammer, probably 55kg (120 lbs) with its attendant hose, is excessive when working on poor ground for it has to be lifted 1.5 — 1.8m (5ft — 6ft) onto the pile which, in windy conditions, will be wobbling about. The piles, each weighing some 22.7kg (50 lb), probably have to be manhandled not only from the main carrying boat to the small flat but then to the bank. After that it is lifted into the clutch of the previous pile. The wood baulk against which the piles are aligned can be floated along from length to length — it holds about fifteen piles — but still has to be lifted up and attached to the kingpost, which is itself manually driven and extracted from the canal bed.

The flat is in situ with the pile-carrier lying on the outside, being unable to get in closer for lack of water. The baulk, kingpost, aligning strut and peg are in the foreground while Roy Turner, a one-time canal employee, is holding up a stake to get the line correct. Stratford-on-Avon canal, 1973.

105. When a crack becomes visible in a wall whether tunnel, bridge or even waterside, common practice was to knock out half-a-brick and then to insert a 'tell-tale' of mortar inscribed with the date. Further movement will split this and the rate of movement can be gauged. Occasionally a string of tell-tales going back 20 or 30 years will show very gradual distortion but here only 14 months separate the tell-tale and photograph.

106. Based on a sketch 'Repairing a Lockgate', Staffordshire & Worcestershire canal around 1800, the tools shown here do not vary greatly from their modern counterparts, with the main exception of the wooden three-legged sheerlegs which finally disappeared — at least for lockgate lifting — on British Waterways Board controlled waterways a decade or so ago, being replaced by a gantry. One assumes a cill is being cut (crosscut saws are, alas, still found occasionally!), the barrow is wooden with an iron-rimmed wheel and the object in the right foreground — a scoop or scope — is only now going out of use, although there still is not really anything quite as efficient for getting rid of water which a pump cannot lift.   A keb (rake), sledgehammer, pick and shovel complete the items then necessary for lock repairs.

J.K. Ebblewhite

107. No details whatsoever are known of this photograph, although the London end of the Grand Junction canal sometime in the 1890s has, quite reasonably, been suggested. It would seem to be posed not only on account of the men's formality but by their excess numbers. Bowlers were commonly worn as safety helmets and the horrible children were and are an inevitable adjunct to canal works. The equipment (except the sheerlegs) and conditions are easily recognised by the men employed on today's stoppages.

108.) Long before a stoppage to exchange lockgates, the order will have been placed with the relevant yard, 109.) or an outside contractor, for new ones of the correct dimensions to be made.   At one time it was commonplace for these to be produced by the local carpenter, but now work is concentrated at certain factory-type depots which, alas, is eliminating the old canal individuality although theoretically cheaper. Once the province of the length foreman, measurement of the old gates is now taken care of by a depot carpenter to eliminate any risk of them being wrong 'hand' or the incorrect height although errors still occur — one of a pair could be made shorter than the other or the collar hole may be too high or too low.   Gates nowadays are either wooden construction with steel strapwork or all-steel with wooden cladding.   Precast

concrete is also possible and no doubt plastic will come one day. Then, of course, the skills depicted here will no longer be necessary. (108) Within Stanley Ferry workshops. The skeleton of one gate destined for Bingley Rise locks on the Leeds & Liverpool canal is lifted up. The mortise hole and the tenon which carry and locate the balance beam are visible above and behind the workman respectively. (109) The tail of a gate carries a pin which is then dropped into a box set in the cill. Both must be exact fits as they decide how close the gate will be to its quoin. Here the carpenter at Stanley Ferry chops out the hole for the pin or pivot. The steel strap prevents shakes or cracks running up the heel post.

Dr. J. Houghton

110. Here at Dowley Gap 2-rise a mobile crane has been used to lift up the old top end gate due for replacement.   The black and white pillars are vertical screw top end ground paddles, typical of this section of the Leeds & Liverpool canal.

Dr. J. Houghton

122

111. A new gate is uplifted by a mobile crane prior to insertion. The paddle-hole at the bottom of the gate is visible, as is the pin hanging down from the heel nearest to the camera.

Dr. J. Houghton

112. The main responsibility for any heavy lock work rested on the capable shoulders of the foreman carpenter; so important were these men to the well-being of a waterway that in wartime they were not released, being classified as essential workers. The late George Bate, B.E.M., Worcester & Birmingham Canal.

113. By contrast with the various mechanical means utilised on British Waterways Board stoppages, people-power is the answer to the problem of lowering a gate at Bulls Lock, Kennet & Avon canal in 1976. This was the first gate made for Bulls Lock by volunteers from the Kennet & Avon Canal Trust and in its workmanship wouldn't have disgraced an old-time carpenter. Rather quirkily and by way of contrast to the sober scene, Granny's old rocking chair is visible on the top left hand corner . . .!

R. Liddiard

114. In the midlands and south in lieu of a mobile crane it has been the normal practice to use a gantry. This had the main advantage that it can be dismantled into relatively small, if heavy and unwieldy, lengths and transported from place to place by boat, whereas the mobile crane is dependant on road access. Erected, it runs on a baulk railway and thus can be moved from end to end of the lock without excessive labour. The hoist is manual and is strenuous work not so much because of the strength required as the gearing reduced the weight, but due to the continual arm over arm action involved. In very frosty weather the drive pulleys may slip on ice or frost necessitating a man climbing up and freeing or propelling it to and fro. It is certainly cold and more than a little eerie perched up there above an empty lock! A carpenter, quite reasonably watched by a labourer, is lifting the new gate out of the boat prior to dropping it into the cut-out in the lockwall. The anchor plate is adjacent to the labourer's Wellington boots, while the white object on the extreme left hand side of the working stage is the new balance beam.

115. Impressionistic study on the Leeds & Liverpool canal. The gates dwarf both the men and their tools.

Dr. J. Houghton

116. Molten lead is used for innumerable purposes around a lock, not least being to hold gate anchors and to bed the locating pins for the quoins into the masonry blocks. Vital, however, is the simple truth that to have molten lead you must have a fire — which canalmen working on a winter stoppage have always appreciated!

Dr. J. Houghton

117. In this photograph the foreman-carpenter is holding the boat in the lock while the old top end (single) gate is lifted on the gantry, waiting to be transferred into the boat. Lying in the open boat is a scrap bottom gate and its balance beam which had been recovered earlier from another lock. The new gate is shown leaning over in the butty boat which has brought it down the flight. Resting on the towpath in the foreground is a set of stop planks while the baulks lying on the grass carry the gantry. Worcester & Birmingham Canal, 1973.

130

119. An impressive contrast with the British Waterways Board stoppage (117, 118) where only five men (including the photographer) were employed. Here over thirty volunteers, under the leadership of Alan Grimster, are involved in the '600' Deepcut Dig, October 8/9, 1977 on the Basingstoke canal. The conditions are abysmal and the equipment primitive but all manner of works, including pointing of brickwork, clearance of debris and removal of a rotten gate are proceeding. The walkway is an upside-down length of Decauville rail — prefabricated units often used by volunteer groups as, given enough hoppers, slurry, rubble and junk can be quickly transported to a tip — grimly reminiscent of wartime trench practice. Lock 16.

A. Lucas

131

120. One of the pleasant features of volunteer works is that not only residents of the area take part but often outsiders whose main interest is the restoration of disused waterways. Here Peter Oates of the Southampton Canal Society is using a lump hammer and bolster to cut out rotten brickwork. Lock 18, Deepcut Flight, Basingstoke Canal, 1977.

A. Lucas

121. In 1952 a breach in the bank of the Leeds & Liverpool canal at Keighley proved to be expensive and difficult to rectify. This photograph, taken when the works were almost finished, shows the gang of stalwarts who were involved, together with a few of their tools. Of all ages, they look happy enough, with an atmospheric background enhancing the scene.

J.K. Ebblewhite

122. By way of contrast with the usual illustrations of workmen this shows them with wives or fiancees on their day off.   Taken at Ludlow, 1927, this would represent about a third of the workmen then employed on the Worcester & Birmingham canal.   At this time such an outing to the Wyre Valley not only represented a day's paid leave but was a further journey than men who had not fought in the 1914-18 war were likely to take under their own steam.   The last such trip organised for the Worcester & Stratford Section men took place only a few years ago; having lost its relevance in this day of the motor car.   The coach is believed to be a Minerva.

The late George Bate, B.E.M.

123. Just once in a while a canal gang can be pinned down for a photographer. Many new works were undertaken on the Grand Union Canal main line in the 1930s, grants being paid towards these by the Government "to relieve distress among the labouring classes". This merry band look happy enough!

INDEX TO NAVIGATIONS